ISBN 780852292 77

HOW TO WRITE A REPORT

John Fletcher is Senior Lecturer in Communication at Slough College. After taking a degree at Oxford, he spent 12 years in commerce and industry, including an office in the City, a shipping company in Singapore, an O & M department in London, and personnel work in Harrogate. At Slough College he has taken classes in writing and other forms of communication for all types of student from catering to management. For many years he has run short courses in effective writing for the Royal Institute of Public Administration, the Institute of Chartered Accountants, and other organizations. This has made him familiar with the many problems that trouble those in mid-career for whom writing is part of their job, but which is tiresome and time-consuming. He has written computer software and video cassette scripts on the skill of writing.

He has read P. G. Wodehouse widely. He is married with four children.

How to Write a Report

John Fletcher

3783010

INSTITUTE OF PERSONNEL MANAGEMENT

Printed and bound in Great Britain by
R J Acford, Chichester

British Library Cataloguing in Publication Data

Fletcher, John
   How to write a report.
   1.   Technical writing
   I.   Title
   808'.0666021   T11
   ISBN 0-85292-277-9

Contents

Introduction

The purpose of this book is to help anyone, particularly in business or any large organization, to write a report.

The larger the organization, the more it depends on the flow of information in writing to the right person at the right time. Some staff, such as systems analysts or research workers, are fully occupied in finding things out and reporting them; the report is the product of their work. Yet for many it is a difficult activity, a skill they have never thoroughly mastered and in which their employers do not provide adequate training.

Such people will, I hope, find the guidance they need here. So will students, particularly if they have to write reports in their examinations. The book covers all kinds of written reports, both inside organizations (investigation, visit or accident report) and between professionals and their clients.

Clearly the advice here cannot replace any specific guidance which an employer gives, but it may be useful to employers who wish to have a basis for their house rules, or to strengthen their report-producing system, or to improve the guidance they give.

The main part of the book assumes that the reader knows the basic grammatical terms. However, these are defined in appendix 2, which may also be useful to those who wish to brush up their basic grammar.

SIX STAGES IN THE LIFE OF A REPORT

1 The writer. A report starts with someone in a particular workplace using particular resources to fashion a report. If the organization does not provide adequate surroundings, equipment and support services, and the writer does not ask for them, the report will probably take more time and money to produce and be a worse product than necessary.

2 The content. From the resources available to him, including notes, books, education, experience and time, the writer chooses

what to put in the report and what to leave out. This is the most intellectually demanding part of his job.

3 The structure. The content has to be arranged in order, with suitable headings and numbering. A relatively small amount of care here can make a vast difference to the appearance and professionalism of the report.

4 The style. Within the structure, the writer has to choose his words and arrange his sentences and paragraphs. The report is then written.

5 The readers. They receive the report, and read some or all of it. They act on it or not, according to their jobs, problems and prejudices, all of which are influenced by how well the report is written.

6 The result. After the report has been read, it can influence events and opinions. By its effect on these the value of a report should finally be judged. Influencing is the real purpose of the report.

1

What is a report?

DEFINITION

The Shorter Oxford English Dictionary has two definitions of 'report' that are of interest.

> An account brought by one person to another, especially of some matter specially investigated.

and

> A formal statement of the results of an investigation, or of any matter on which definite information is required, made by some person or body instructed or required to do so.

The second definition would be enough by itself except that some reports are written on the writer's own initiative and not to someone else's instructions, so the first broader definition is useful as well.

Most people at some point in their working lives are required to write a report. Reports can be long or short, regular or 'one-offs'. They may take the form of letters, memoranda or a narrative broken up by headings. Some will be based on an investigation, some an account of a meeting or discussion.

This book aims to help readers who want to write their reports, whatever form they may take and whatever topic they cover, precisely and effectively.

Reports are written to record, to inform and to recommend. This does not define the purposes of a report fully, as chapter 2 shows, but it is a useful starting point.

Written or spoken

While this book is concerned with reports in writing, a spoken report often precedes or follows a written one. For example, an investigator may submit a written report to members of a committee to read in advance of the meeting. He then goes to the meeting to support his report with a spoken presentation, explaining matters, answering questions, reporting on matters not possible or suitable to put in writing. Or the other way round: an auditor meets a client and discusses a change in some procedure and knows how far the client is likely to accept his proposals. He then writes a report to confirm the discussion and note points of agreement, and the difficulties. This combination of written and spoken reports has the advantages of both methods. The spoken part is quick and likely to be cheaper, and enables many subtle nuances to be communicated; the written part can be copied and distributed widely, and provides a long term record.

Regular or one-off

Many reports are produced at regular intervals to form a series. Examples are daily quality control reports, weekly cash flow reports, monthly turnover reports and annual company reports.

Regular short reports usually look like forms, with preset headings and 'boxes' for the variable information. The author, or 'completer', of the report has little preparation to do. Readers can find the information they want quickly and can easily compare any report with its predecessor in the series because the layout is identical. These advantages are so great that regular reports should be turned into forms where possible. But in annual reports the variation from year to year will normally make it necessary to vary the layout.

The drawback of regular reports and forms in business is that they are designed at one time, for particular readers and purposes, and may continue to be used long after readers and purposes have changed. It is always easier to say 'this is how we did it last time; we'll follow that' than to work out the best way of doing it now.

One-off reports do not have that disadvantage; the writer knows he must think about each report afresh. This remains true even though the writer may produce many reports at frequent intervals, all similar, but one-off to the reader. For instance, a work study officer will write many work study reports, to a similar pattern and even with some identical information. But each will have different readers, purposes, headings and content, for which he needs the developed skills of report writing, which are the subject of this book.

Professional people, such as lawyers, accountants, surveyors and consultants, reporting to clients know the report will be a one-off for the client and so the report must be complete in itself, stating the purpose each time. Regular reports do not necessarily do this.

APPEARANCE AND STRUCTURE

The first kind of report with which most people are familiar is the school report with headings down the left side and boxes on the right, in which comments are handwritten. It could be called a form, and indeed many reports at work are forms. Quality control reports, routine laboratory test reports and regular management accounts are all some kind of form. The size of the boxes may vary, but like the headings, the author of the variable information has no control over the space at his disposal. Readers can find the information they want quickly and can easily compare one report with another. The advantages of a form over a report where the writer has to choose the headings and decide how much to write under each are great, as already described, although it is not always possible to use a form where the amount to be written under each heading varies from report to report.

Telephone messages are the simplest reports. Information is standard. The reader needs to know the name and number of the caller, the date and time of the call, the name of the person who took it and the substance of the message. Many telephone messages are so similar that forms are often used for this purpose.

Other internal messages are memoranda. There may be headings on the memorandum form for entering standard information: From, To, Date, Subject, to ensure that these are not forgotten. Quite long reports can be sent as memoranda.

External reports may use the format of letters, beginning 'Dear . . .' and ending 'Yours . . .' or more plain reports without the courtesies of a letter but using only functional headings. In certain professions, such as law and accountancy, letters are still used to contain a report, but the longer the report the more artificial these letter formalities seem and it is increasingly common to have simply a covering letter (which may summarize the report) and to leave the report to stand alone.

PURPOSE

Record, inform, recommend: these are the purposes of a report. But a report written to recommend will have to do the other two things as well: record and inform. A report 'for information only' will record and may include recommendations to be carried out by someone other than the person to whom it is 'for information'. But information is not passed on for its own sake. It does affect people and someone receiving a report 'for information' may well decide to take some action after reading it. Even a report written purely 'for the record' assumes that someone, some day, might be influenced by it, might need the record to decide something, otherwise it is pointless. One of the purposes might in fact be expressed as follows:

> This is a complicated matter which I have mastered with some difficulty. I can put it in writing now. If I wait until someone asks for the information before writing the report, I shall have forgotten it, or have other things to do, or be on holiday, sick, in another job or dead. So I will write it now 'for the record'.

2

How to define the purpose and audience

RELEVANCE

People who are accustomed to reading reports usually find it easier
to become skilful report writers themselves. The difference between
this kind of work and English at school and college is clear: you are
more likely to have at least some idea of what makes a report fail or
succeed; and you will, above all, know that other people's reports
can be boring. You may not know the causes of a report being dull
or unconvincing, but you will know well enough that many reports
are, indeed, exactly that.

If you have to write a report without the experience of having
read or written one before, you can find Royal Commission reports
to read in a public library. If you are a manager you will know that
you cannot do your job without reports and will be unlikely to be in
your post for long without at least a few experiences of writing
them. You will also have read them or thrown them away on many
occasions. Why is report writing so difficult?

Fundamentally, it is because people are too casual. This is shown
above all in what could be called the 'oh, by the way' approach. A
senior executive stops his subordinate in the corridor and says 'are
you free on Thursday? Good. I wonder if you could go along to the
Machine Tools Exhibition and have a look at what's on offer? Let
me have a report when you come back'. The subordinate dutifully
attends the exhibition, which is interesting and enjoyable enough.
He collects written material from a range of manufacturers and
some documents put out by the organizers. When he gets back to
the office he starts his report. As he has no idea what the report is
wanted for, but he has the impression that he ought to show that
his time was not wasted, he makes a fairly full report. No

manufacturer and few exhibits are omitted. He may spend a little more time on those exhibits which interested him and rather less on those where he paid only a fleeting visit, but at least no one can accuse him of not having gone and no one can accuse him of not having brought back plenty of information. The result is chaos and wasted time. It is chaos because, apart from proving that he attended, there is no useful purpose served by the report. The information is not organized. It is not directed towards anyone taking a decision. It is too long and the various sections of the report do not hang together in any organized, logical fashion.

It is wasted time because it has taken him considerable time to write and will take others a great deal of time to read even if they read it only to discover that there was nothing in it of significance for them. This wasted time can be reduced by experienced report readers who will glance through the document quickly and throw it away; but it remains a waste of paper and typing.

A good report is good, not just in the writing, not just in the reading, but in the thought that it provokes and the decisions that it makes possible.

Think of the good reports that you have read: it is unlikely that you were delighted with the elegance of the author's style, though reports produced expensively with glossy paper and coloured illustrations can naturally be impressive, but it is likely that the report was a help to you in some part of your work. For example, a report on labour turnover may be good or bad. If it is exactly the same as the previous report on labour turnover with only a few different figures in corresponding places it is doubtful whether it will be any use. If, on the other hand, it pinpoints where some investigation or action may be required and produces figures to support that investigation or action, it is at least trying to be constructive.

The most important question that a report writer has to ask himself is 'what is irrelevant?', what to omit. It is also the most difficult question, since the writer must establish who the readers are and what they will need in order to use the report, in other words, its purpose.
Ask yourself this question when you are considering what to put in the report:

What should I put into the mind of my readers so that they can use the report for its intended purpose?

The way the mind of the reader and the purpose of the document interlock is one of the themes running through all business writing. It affects many documents besides reports and within a report it can be applied on quite a small scale. A good exercise is to ask yourself of some tiny part of the report, for example the date on the title page:

> Why is this necessary? What decision is going to be taken on the basis of this information, the date? What kind of readers are going to read the date?

If you follow the logic through, you will find at least two reasons. First, it establishes the currency of the information it contains. Secondly, reports are likely to be filed in date order, and when someone requests the retrieval of the report from the filing system, possibly quite some time later, it may well be vaguely described as 'that report on the machine tool exhibition written about eight or nine months ago'. Readers include filing clerks and unknown people in what might be called 'posterity'.

So if the job of identifying the readers is difficult, the job of defining the purpose is equally difficult. The 'Oh, by the way' approach is much easier than tackling these problems, but it also leads to confusion and time wasting. If reports are to be relevant, close attention has to be paid to the purpose, explained below, and to the readers, discussed on pages 10 to 13.

DEFINING THE PURPOSE

If you ask yourself 'Why am I writing this report?' there are two kinds of answers. One purpose refers to the past. The other refers to the future. For instance:

(i) you may be writing a report on your visit to the exhibition because your boss asked you to

(ii) or you may be writing a report on the exhibition because in the next month your firm will have to decide which of various pieces of equipment to order.

These two kinds of purposes are not incompatible; both are valid and they are complementary. To start preparing a report solely on the basis of knowing the first purpose without being aware of the second plainly lessens its value to the reader.

Are you writing a report at the moment? If so, write down its purpose. Probably it will embrace one or more of the purposes listed in chapter 1: to record, to inform, to recommend. But these intermediate purposes cannot be the end of the story. The real purpose of a report is the outcome, or result, or the action that should be taken after the report is read.

The interdependence of these purposes is crucial in effective report writing; events should not be recorded purely for the fun of it, nor should you inform people simply because they are ignorant, nor should you make recommendations simply because it is the conventional way to end a report. Reports are part of a system in which people do their work, and they should help them to do it better; for example, to take better decisions.

It may not be easy to pin down what the precise outcome will be. If you are writing a report about an exhibition for 'posterity', in case over the following year someone is interested in a piece of equipment, the outcome is so unknown that the purpose is perhaps as well left as 'record'. But the more you can identify who might ask for the report and what they might be interested in, the more useful your report is likely to be.

If you are making recommendations, your report needs to specify the reasons for them, the means by which they can be achieved and the outcome that can be expected. If you begin your purpose with 'to enable . . .' you are likely to ensure that you do enable your reader to do something (and not merely recommend him to do it).

One report may have many readers and many purposes. One way of enabling each reader to use the report for his own purpose is to have different sections corresponding to different readers and purposes. This is why the purposes have to be defined carefully before the structure of the report is planned. If one reader and purpose is to be given priority, then the report should say so. In a good report it is easy to find a statement of purpose, either under the heading 'Terms of reference' or 'Purpose' or 'Introduction'. The author should put this in even if there is only one reader of importance, who is perfectly well aware of the purpose of the report. Every writer should assume that a report will be read by people other than those for whom it was primarily intended. These others will not know the purpose of the report and may consequently criticize it as inadequate, unless its purpose, scope and limitations are stated fully. Such a statement also 'fixes' the report for posterity so that if another manager is asked to report on a related subject, or your successor is asked years afterwards to update your report, the scope of your work can be identified quickly.

TERMS OF REFERENCE

This phrase is normally used by Royal Commissions to describe the assignment they are given. It is commonly accepted that for such an official document involving considerable public expenditure a great deal of care is needed with the statement of what the Royal Commission is expected to do, and why. In fact, it is possible to look at terms of reference in another way as well: they cover the information that the writer needs to know before he starts. All report writers should have a checklist of information they require before starting or the report may be unfairly criticized or censored, since the criticism will be based on lack of information or even wrong information.

It is unfortunately a general truth that those who ask their subordinates in business to write reports do not always give them all the information they will need. The writer is more likely to think through what he needs to know than the person giving him the assignment. The onus must therefore rest on the writer of the report to fill any blanks in his knowledge by asking. The first question, then, is the 'purpose' as discussed previously. The readership will normally be implied in the purpose; but if it is not obvious from the purpose who the readers are, then they need to be explicitly identified.

Secondly, the scope and limits of the report. The scope includes those items which are uppermost in the mind of the person who has commissioned the report, the particular areas that the report should cover; the limits specify any areas or matters which are excluded. There may well be occasions on which a writer is asked not to cover a certain subject.

Thirdly, there are some matters on which the writer must be properly briefed, but which it may not be necessary to put in writing and certainly not in the report. These include the deadline, or time which the writer has available for collecting information, assessing it and writing the report; the expected length of the report; and other resources such as money and man hours, which he is authorized and enabled to use. In certain cases, it may be necessary for him to have access to documents which would be otherwise confidential and he may need to be assured of this in writing.

Fourthly, there is information too sensitive to write down, but which may be nonetheless important. For example, information about personalities, political attitudes, matters of long term board policy and questions whose nuance can be conveyed only at a private meeting or which it would be contrary to the common interest to put in writing. It should be obvious that the writer should have an interview before he begins where such matters can be discussed. Information obtained in the first two questions, that is purpose and readership, and scope and limits, should be stated as terms of reference early on in the report. Information elicited by the third and fourth questions will not be specified in that statement.

The stated terms of reference enable the writer to decide what is relevant and to check that no gap is left in his argument. They establish the criteria by which the report is to be judged and edited.

WHAT YOU NEED TO KNOW ABOUT THE READERS

It is clear that the writer needs to know who his readers are and something about them to establish what is relevant in the report. The extent to which readers are known affects how difficult or how much easier it is to write for them. Writing to strangers is laborious, the result does not always flow easily and it frequently fails to achieve the right result. On the other hand, writing to people you know is enjoyable, enables you to express yourself more freely and is in every sense more effective. If you do not know your reader you have less common ground. You cannot assume a common understanding of the problem or a common interest in its solution. You must write in a simple way lest the reader is uninformed and at the same time achieve the opposite: write in a polished, sophisticated way in case the reader is well informed. The writer has to cater for all possibilities.

First of all, the writer needs to know the reader's language. Apart from the obvious difficulty of writing to those with a different native tongue, there are subtle differences between various kinds of English. Those regularly reading papers from, or writing to, Americans will be familiar with different idioms and usages.

Although English is widely understood by those who have a different first language, a report for them may have to be written in a different way from one which is going only to those brought up in

10

England. And of those with an English upbringing, clearly there are differences between the language of those whose pleasure is to read the 'leaders' in the small circulation 'quality' press and those whose preference is for the mass circulation press. Again many reports are technical and the writer needs to ask himself how much of the technical language has been mastered by his reader. The word 'jargon' has arisen because writers are often unaware of the difference of language between themselves and their readers.

If possible, a writer should find out something about the readers' 'frame of reference'. This (nothing to do with terms of reference) is the window through which everyone looks out on the world. Human beings are not tape recorders or cameras who simply record exactly what is put in front of them, but have brains that pose questions while reading a document, probing as they go to find answers. Readers pass over information that seems to have no bearing on their questions, and may even deny the evidence was there; but where a word or phrase shows that the reader may expect to find an answer to his question, it may lead him into imagining he sees the answer when in fact no direct answer is given at all.

The frame of reference leads on to a wide field, which includes the reader's attitudes, priorities and prejudices. In a business report it is useful to distinguish between those for whom the prime loyalty is to their colleagues or the prime loyalty is to efficiency; or between those for whom work study is a problem and those for whom it is a solution.

If the report writer is trying to persuade someone to take a particular course of action, then it is important to know whether that course of action is one which the reader is likely to agree with in any event. If so, the writer need not argue at length. But if the reader is disposed to disagree, then the writer must find out the basis of disagreement and deal with the objections, using whatever arguments will be most effective with that particular reader.

Every reader has emotion and imagination. No report is read by a disembodied brain. Those engaged in persuading other people professionally, such as advertisers and politicians, find it much more effective to appeal to feelings, to establish a sense of confidence in the writer and possibly to attack the reader's confidence in others, rather than to present a purely rational argument. This is not to suggest that rational argument can be omitted, but that the reader's emotions must be considered as well. If your reader's head

11

is convinced but his heart is alienated, you have lost the argument.

The imagination is different from the emotions: the reader's imagination is what enables him to construct mental pictures or images of your proposal. If you are proposing to redesign a motorway the role of the imagination is obvious. If you are discussing the sales of the last quarter expressed in product groups and areas, the role of the imagination is not so clear. In fact, if you express this in a complicated table most people's imagination will not come into play at all, which is why such tables are commonly skipped or misunderstood.

If, however, you present a graph or histogram of the same information, the imagination has a picture or image already presented to it which it can grasp easily and, with most people, can remember for a long time. This is why such pictorial ways of presenting abstract information enable most people to understand quite complex trends immediately and without conscious effort. It is why speakers who use visual aids are remembered more readily, and why abstract nouns, which the imagination cannot grasp without misrepresentation make heavy, difficult reading (*see* chapter 5, page 27).

How to find out

Much the best way to find out the information you need to know about your readers is to meet them. The difference between writing to readers before and after meeting them has been described and this goes some way towards explaining why meeting them is so useful. Many people automatically absorb characteristics of their readers on meeting them and are able, again without thinking too closely about it, to adapt their writing to make allowances for them.

The level of a person's language comes across primarily in how he speaks, but it may also be apparent from what he reads, or from material he has in his office. It is not difficult in conversation to test the reader's technical vocabulary by using words and seeing from the reaction whether further explanation is required, or even by asking directly whether he is familiar with this or that technical term.

If you cannot meet your reader the next best method of finding the information you need about him is by telephone or by reading correspondence or other written work he has produced. Of these two, there is no doubt that the telephone is better.

Occasionally, a writer will have to write for readers abroad where direct contact is not practicable. There is, however, one piece of information about an individual which can be used advantageously. You nearly always know, or can easily discover, the occupation or job of your readers. It is often possible to make accurate deductions not only about a person's technical ability, education and training, but also his attitudes, priorities and prejudices, if you know his occupation.

Thus, a problem about the best method of manufacturing a component will be an engineering problem to an engineer, a mechanical engineering problem to a mechanical engineer, a problem in staff relations to a personnel officer, a problem in costs to an accountant, and no doubt something different to every different occupation.

Making assumptions in this way, however, is much less satisfactory than direct contact since it is absurd to presume that all members of one occupation share a similar outlook and experience. It is nevertheless better than nothing.

What if there are many readers with different occupations, priorities, languages etc? Page 8 discusses a similar problem relating to a report which has many purposes, and what applies to purposes applies here to readers. It may be that there is one reader who is more important than all the others put together and it may be possible, therefore, to concentrate on writing a report tailored to his particular needs. If that is not possible, it is likely that the report will become long, with different sections and appendices related to the needs of different individuals. Where the problem concerns differences of language, either a glossary must be provided, as an appendix, or the language used must be the simplest, least technical which the reader can understand. The drawback of preparing a report which the more educated reader may find lacking in specialist terms is balanced by holding the attention of other readers by whom the jargon would not be understood. It is important to keep your readers with you.

3

How to prepare for writing

How important is the work of writing?

Many organizations scarcely regard writing as work at all. These organizations, particularly those primarily engaged in research, plan investigations, surveys and other detailed studies, carefully calculate the time and budget which will be required for the research but allow no time or budget for writing the report. It is as though writing were some kind of universal pleasure which employees were lucky to be allowed to do; or alternatively as if producing a brilliant report were so easy and quick by comparison with the rest of the work that its effect on the timing and costing could be ignored. Commonly the view is held that writing is not 'real work'; it is a nuisance activity which interrupts the real work.

These sentiments are held even in organizations where the report is the only visible product that the customer sees for the money which enables the 'real' work to continue. They are also, but less surprisingly, common in organizations where there are constant complaints that the writing is bad. Writing must be treated like the hard work it is and respected accordingly.

Costing a report

One mark of the importance an organization attaches to the work of writing is the extent to which it appears in the balance sheet as part of the costs of an activity. Management should know the cost of each activity for which they are responsible. At the completion of a project the advance estimates are compared with the real costs incurred. With reports as with other jobs, costs are a combination of several elements: man-hours, materials and production costs. It is useful to have a notional hourly rate for each employee involved. This normally begins with author and typist, and may include

14

others: superiors, colleagues, an editor, graphic designer or illustrator, a photocopier operator, a collator and so on. It is simple to calculate the cost of materials which is principally paper, and most companies use an established in-company price list for photocopied pages. Despite the widespread fear that estimating itself is time-consuming and costly, it can be done quickly. Before completing many reports the writer has built up useful knowledge to apply as a formula for the costs of future reports. If travel agents estimate the cost of booking one holiday, and governments the cost of building a motorway, there cannot be a report too short or too long to cost.

THE USE OF MACHINES

Technology has brought many aids to writing as it has to other activities in industry. Organizations which use dictating machines extensively for correspondence and recording data during visits to sites, assembly lines and so on, often fail to encourage their use for reports. Similarly, British companies are using word processors more frequently for compiling, maintaining and storing stock details, but their value to writers and editors often goes unrecognized. Perhaps it is better to ignore them than to over-use them and to put a report through a dozen editions simply because it seems so easy; but there is a happy mean.

The most obvious reason for using a dictating machine is economy; there is a second one, that it forces you to plan your work, at least in outline, before writing.

Dictating machines themselves did not cost much even before the explosion in electronic technology. Pocket dictating machines cost a negligible proportion of the cost of the time they can save. Dictating is quicker than writing in pen and ink. An audio-typist can type from a tape more quickly than from the average longhand manuscript. Shorthand dictation costs the time of the shorthand typist taking it and waiting while the dictator crystallizes his thoughts or while he deals with interruptions.

The second and greater argument for using dictating machines is that in any document except the shortest the dictator has to make a list of points before he starts to avoid constant erasure and re-dictation. Planning the sequence of the material has to be the first task and dictating machines oblige him to do this thoroughly. To ensure effective understanding between the dictator and the typist, it is useful for the two to meet so that the

15

background can be explained and any preferred work habits can be outlined, such as slow or fast delivery or punctuation specified or left to the intelligence of the typist. The dictator can also make any requests relating to house style, spacing, number of copies and so on although these instructions should also be dictated at the beginning of the tape as a reminder.

BENEFITS OF WORD PROCESSORS (WPs)

Although by no means universally installed in British organizations, word processors, part of the 'micro computer revolution', are rapidly gaining ground on the traditional typewriter for a number of office functions, one of them being the typing, editing and printing of reports. Organizations in the vanguard of the WP revolution have tended to be law practices, quantity surveying and management consultancies, where reports are the bread and butter of their business.

The underlying principle of a WP is that information, or the draft report, is typed on a keyboard (a sophisticated version of the traditional typewriter with a number of extra keys) and recorded in magnetic form, on a disc or tape, where it is stored indefinitely until revised or deleted. The information can be reproduced automatically whenever required and can be reviewed on a screen, or visual display unit (VDU).

Once the draft report has been keyed in, and a copy printed out, the writer can edit, revise and have any corrections made rapidly. Even major rewrites or the insertion of extra paragraphs do not necessitate a complete retyping of the report, since the WP can automatically realign and repaginate the entire text. The layout, length and spacing of lines and paragraphs can also be revised with great ease. This text editing facility is a major WP benefit for report writers, editors and typists. When the report is complete, copies can be printed off speedily and the original, safely stored on the disc, can be used in the future for additional copies if required.

One drawback to WPs which should not be overlooked is the opportunity they present to succumb to the temptation to make repeated improvements to the report; the ease with which the text can be edited, revised and reprinted can prolong the completion and thereby raise the cost of a report. Perfectionist beware.

THE USE OF TIME

In many jobs there is a certain amount of 'dead time' which can be used for planning reports. Those who use dictating machines can work in airport lounges or even in trains to capture the telling phrase as it occurs to them so as not to lose it. It is not recommended, however, as the right environment.

While it is important to control the backlog of other work, it is equally important to control the pressure that this and preparing the report places on the writer. Most people work to deadlines: that is, work is produced at the last possible minute. Only the knowledge that the work cannot be delayed forces the writer to concentrate.

While too little pressure is wasteful, too much leads to ulcers. There is a point beyond which pressure cannot go without leading to collapse. Again it is important for writers to know how much work they can reasonably do in a given time. When there is too much, the solution is managerial; delegating work to subordinates, or re-allocating it between colleagues. Again here it is important to know how much time a given job can be reasonably expected to take.

The process of time control may include four stages:

(1) Setting the target. This should be an amount of time considered reasonable for doing a specific job. It should not be solely related to the quantity of writing, because verbose writing is wasteful. One of the most important stages in producing a document comes when the writer is cutting out unnecessary words.

(2) Noting the actual starting and finishing times of each parcel of measured work. This could be recorded in a diary, for instance, or, for a draft report, in a covering note giving the document's history during its gestation.

(3) A record should be kept of the variation or variance between target and actual times.

(4) At regular intervals such as weekly or monthly it is important to analyse the variances. Where a job turns out to be taking a longer or shorter time than was estimated, the fault lies either in the estimating or the doing. Regular analysis of variances enables people either to work better by drawing attention to excessive delays, or to estimate more precisely. Accurate estimating is essential both for planning the work of the individual and for integrating the work of a team.

WORKING CONDITIONS

Good working conditions are as necessary for writing as for any other form of manufacturing. The fact that writing is not costed is no doubt one reason why few organizations have bothered to plan the ideal working environment for a report writer.

(a) Environment

Most commonly, organizations expect employees to do their writing at a desk in their office, but this simple requirement overlooks the special considerations that apply to the act, and the art, of writing.

Interior decorators do sometimes have a refreshing influence on office design, taking into account the choice of wall colours and the effect of natural or artificial light. The design of some desks and chairs is tailored to comfort and convenience but the dominant factor in office design is frequently a simple question of squashing the maximum number of people into the smallest space. Where double glazing is installed it is more likely to be in the interests of saving fuel costs than eliminating external noise. These factors and others which affect the efficiency and concentration of a report writer have not had their proper influence on the design of his place of work.

One difficulty is that different people require a different environment; for instance, some work better with background music while others prefer quiet. Of course, it is not always desirable to introduce music into an office where it will disturb others. It may be necessary to arrange to do your writing in some more congenial place.

(b) Peace and quiet

Interruptions need to be minimized. They are wasteful since the writer has to pick up the threads again after they have been dealt with. It may be easy to read to the end of a sentence in a book and return immediately to the correct place or mark the point in the addition of a column of figures. But interruptions to a sustained piece of report planning or writing can completely disrupt the logic in a train of thought. Time has to be spent going through the steps again. Perhaps that perfect turn of phrase which has crystal-

18

lized in the mind but not yet reached the paper will never come again.

Interruptions also add to the time scale and costs of the report, and while it is very valuable to be able to brake, change direction suddenly, accelerate rapidly, and then return to the first route, interruptions often eat away the time allocated for your own work.

Interruptions mainly are the telephone, the uninvited intrusion and the presence of others in the same office. These can be dealt with quickly by simply accepting no calls or leaving the receiver off the hook, and hanging a notice on your door or desk requesting 'DO NOT DISTURB'. Possibly a screen around your desk will deter intruders.

(c) Location and access

While comfort and freedom from interruption are two important factors in choosing your writing location, there are others which should not be overlooked: the necessity for colleagues to have access to you in an emergency; the location you choose should be acceptable to and fit in with others; and documents which you may need to refer to in writing your report should be near to hand. It may be possible to find a vacant interview room (where the lack of interruption is recognized) or the room of an absent colleague, or simply to take work home, provided the environment there does in fact meet all these requirements. (There, of course, the problem of access to colleagues and documents is more acute.) Nevertheless, a suitable working environment has to be found and it is essential to establish at the planning stage of the report where you will do your writing, and to make arrangements accordingly.

4

How to structure a report

WHY AND WHEN TO DRAFT THE STRUCTURE

Before sitting down to draft the report, the writer needs to decide on the sequence of headings by which he is going to lead the reader through the entire project. Clarifying the structure in this way should not take long and makes a great difference to the appearance and readability of the report.

In many organizations, experience has shown that it saves time and tempers if the writer and the person who commissioned the report agree on the structure before the first word is written. In fact, the structure should be drafted twice: first, when the terms of reference have been established and before the investigation has started; and secondly, when the investigation has been completed and the findings may require some revision of the initial structure. Preparing a first draft structure has three advantages: it ensures that there is no misunderstanding on the part of the writer about the terms of reference; the writer sets out with a structure that is likely to be close to what the reader is expecting when he receives the report; and it is easier to take the provisional structure and revise it in the light of the investigation than to start at that stage with a blank sheet on to which a collection of various facts, figures and ideas have to be presented in a logical order.

THE READERS' INFLUENCE ON STRUCTURE

Start by thinking about what happens to your report when you have finished with it.

Postmen and messengers deliver it. The reader identifies it from the other material in his in-tray, takes it and reads it. He does not necessarily read all of it nor in the order in which you have written it. He may be interested in the detail in some aspects but not in others. Before taking any action he has to consider what that action might be, what difficulties there may be to overcome and which other people to persuade. He may need to discuss it with another colleague. If you have made recommendations he has to meet your request, possibly by asking others to carry out some task, possibly by dictating a letter or memorandum. He has to file your report, in such a way that if he wants to refer to it a month later, or if someone else asks for it a year later, it is easily identified and retrieved.

The reason why you should think about all these things before starting to write is that each of them can affect the way you present your report. Many of the points have a bearing on the sequence of headings, or structure, of the report. Most obviously a clear set of headings enables the reader to identify the parts he is interested in and the order in which to read them.

Specimen structure

A logical and conventional sequence of headings for a long report might be as follows:

title
summary
list of contents
introduction
body of report under headings
conclusions
recommendations
appendices.

Title

The title page should help the postmen and messengers, the filing clerks and those trying to identify and retrieve the report subsequently. It may include the title, subtitle, who the report is by, who the report is to, the report's date, the name of the issuing organization, reference numbers and degree of confidentiality.

Since the title of the report is to be used to identify it, the main point is that it should not resemble the title of any other report. It may be that the report will be referred to in committee and elsewhere and for this purpose a short title is ideal. A subtitle is useful if it is impossible for the same title to be both short enough for reference and specific enough to avoid confusion.

Summary

The summary of a report has two intended purposes and readers: it should help the busy managing director who has not time to read anything else, and it should also help those who do intend to read the whole report but would appreciate a précis first. For both purposes the summary needs to be brief and appear early in the sequence. Some organizations actually place the summary on the title page and this seems perfectly logical.

There are two customary lengths of summary: one paragraph (50 to 100 words) and one page (300 to 400 words). The paragraph-length summary is appropriate when, as in scientific circles, summaries from large numbers of reports are published together separated from the reports they summarize. The one-page summary seems customary for commercial purposes.

The summary is a précis of the whole report and not merely of the conclusions or recommendations, although it will clearly include these. It will also include such statement of the purpose, or significant pieces of evidence, as will help the summary-reader.

Table of contents

This is a list of chapters or sections, in the same sequence as they occur in the report, giving also the number of the chapter or section and the page on which it begins. It is unnecessary in a short report, but in a long report helps the reader to see the scope of the report and find quickly the section he wishes to read next. It is often called simply 'Contents' and must be distinguished from an 'Index', which is a list of all the main points discussed (not only the headings) in alphabetical order (not the order in which they occur). Indexes conventionally come at the back, and are useful in books but unusual in commercial reports.

Introduction

In a book this may be separate from the main part of the text, and is often skipped by those who intend to read all the rest. In a report it is commonly the heading given to certain essential preliminaries which are not weighty enough to have a heading of their own. These include:

the events leading up to the request for a report, or other background history

the terms of reference, giving the purpose, scope, and limits of the report

the resources available to the report writer such as staff, time, and the authority to collect evidence

the method of collecting evidence and the principal sources

acknowledgements of help received

a definition of terms used, or a reference to a glossary where the reader can find such definitions.

The body of the report

The headings in the middle of the report are not standard. The report writer has to invent them himself, and the skill with which he does so will have a disproportionate effect on the report's quality. He should consider the following points.

The heading should be one the readers expect, or failing that, which they can at least interpret correctly. To ensure they are what the reader expects, it is good to set out a 'headings plan' after receiving terms of reference but before collecting evidence. To ensure that they can be interpreted correctly, they need to be checked against the text beneath each one. Taken together, the headings should enable the reader to find any one particular answer he is looking for. They must cover the ground. Headings should not overlap, in the sense that headings on the same level should cover distinct ground. But the same piece of evidence may appear twice, because it is significant in two different ways, and so has to go under two headings.

Most readers do not read the report in exactly the order in which the writer lays it out, because they have different interests. Make sure the headings are precise enough to tell the reader what is in each: headings such as 'General' or 'Other considerations' are useless.

At the same time the headings need to be in a logical order. Sometimes this will mean in chronological order; sometimes in order of importance; sometimes going from the long-term to the short-term, or the general to the particular; sometimes in alphabetical order. The main point about a logical order is that it should be what the reader will find logical.

When headings and subheadings are used, the heading applies to all the subheadings underneath it. So if the main heading is 'Flowers', under which there are subheadings 'English. Welsh. Scottish.' there is no need to say 'English Flowers'.

Headings should be short, subject to the previous points. The number of headings will depend on the length of the material to be divided. Between three and six headings a page is acceptable to most people; but the more complex the material (for instance, with instructions) the more headings the reader will appreciate.

Conclusions

The conclusions of a report are the critical part, in the sense that it is here that the author delivers his verdict. He may recapitulate evidence which he has already described in the body of the report to show how it has helped him reach a judgement. Frequently it will involve comparing different possibilities and therefore it is likely to be written in flowing prose, or more like an essay than other parts of the report.

As well as looking back to the evidence, it looks forward to the recommendations and gives the reasons for one course of action rather than another. Conclusions have to be persuasive; the reader must go along with the writer and be convinced by the argument.

Recommendations

Recommendations are best written as though they were to be detached from the report and given to some robot who needed to know exactly what to do, but not why. Only in this way can the recommendations be kept as crisp and short as possible, avoiding any overlap with the conclusions. Even so they may be a long list. If they are, it is worth subdividing them, for instance into long term and short term, or by the different people or agencies who should implement them.

Appendices

Appendices contain technical information for specialist readers and are presented in a way that will make it easy for the others to skip.

They may therefore be very long; there is nothing wrong in an appendix being longer than the rest of the report.

They are put at the end of the other information to emphasize that they are for specialists only and that the report makes sense without them. They may include, for instance, a list of sources, or bibliography; they frequently include tables and diagrammatic material too bulky to be conveniently reproduced in the main body of the text. Where there are many technical terms used in the report, well known to some readers but unknown to others, the last appendix may be a glossary.

NUMBERING

Some form of numbering is essential for ease of reference. The traditional commercial system is to number headings with arabic numerals, 1, 2, 3, and subheadings with letters, (a), (b), (c). If a third layer is required, roman numerals are available (i), (ii), (iii). Increasingly this has been replaced by the 1.1, or 'decimal system', which uses arabic numerals for all layers of headings, for example in engineering companies.

Another form of numbering is not to number the headings, but only the paragraphs and then in sequence from the beginning of the report to the end, irrespective of the heading they come under. This is common in Royal Commission reports and other civil service documents.

It may be necessary to design a system of numbers appropriate for your own particular document, but it is better if an organization decides on its number system, as part of 'house style' for its own purposes and for all reports.

Three layers of numbers, such as 1 (a) (i) are enough. If there is a fourth layer, the numbering system is more likely to confuse than to help, and the writer should see whether his structure is not itself too intricate to follow. Probably the answer is to reorganize the headings and to have more main headings.

One cause of excessive layers of headings is the use of a heading, such as 'Investigation', to cover all the material between the Introduction and Conclusion. This not only adds an unnecessary layer to the central and complicated part of the report, but the heading tells the reader nothing useful about the sections beneath.

IS IT READABLE?

The following questions* will help to check that the report is easy to read.

(i) Who is the report for? Have you a clear idea of the readership and is the report directed to the right audience?

(ii) Are the opening paragraphs clear, short and relevant? Pay special attention to them.

(iii) Have you defined the problem concisely in words that the readers will understand?

(iv) Are your decisions and proposals presented in a neutral and thoughtful way?

(v) Are your sentences and paragraphs relatively short? If the average length of your sentences is more than 25 words, most people will find them difficult to read. A paragraph with more than 14 to 20 lines can be overpowering.

(vi) Have you tried out your report on a 'guinea pig' to discover what its faults might be?

(vii) Have you tried to eliminate or at least minimize jargon? Even a technical report can be unnecessarily jargon-ridden.

(viii) Is the report too long? Most management reports over 10 pages are capable of being shortened with considerable gain in reader interest, understanding, persuasiveness.

---

* (Adapted by kind permission from Leigh A. *Decisions, Decisions.* London, Institute of Personnel Management, 1983).

5

How to make a report readable

WHAT MAKES A DOCUMENT ATTRACTIVE?

The first impact a report or other working document makes does not depend on words, unless those words are written in letters so large as to be called the work of a layout specialist rather than an author.

In the fields of marketing and journalism one or more highly skilled individuals choose the paper, look after the colour, the white spaces around paragraphs and pages of text, select typography and do other similar jobs which create atmosphere and make it visually pleasing. This is the contribution that publishers make to their books. No doubt it can be counter-productive when the reader is conscious of it but in moderation it has two important uses.

Functionally, it helps the reader to understand and remember the message. Thus, a coloured photograph or graph or histogram conveys complex messages swiftly and easily. Secondly, it is polite: it should demonstrate to the reader that the author is interested in him and has taken trouble to make his job as easy as possible.

But the average report writer has no layout specialist to advise him. For the most part his reports are, at best, A4 typescript. He is lucky if he works in an organization where there are house rules about the width of margins or specially designed covers which he can use for his reports. Often the rules or guidelines for typists are introduced by work study specialists who have more interest in saving typing time than in the elegance or appearance of the finished document. But almost any such guideline, which is seriously discussed in advance and then applied consistently, will have the effect of making the documents concerned more attractive.

The ordinary author can look at the methods and techniques used around him. Newspapers, circulars, advertising material all use different methods to get their message across, and if he is willing to spend a while analysing how it is done and which methods are successful, he may be able to adopt some of the methods of the specialist.

While he is looking at the layout methods he might also consider the words that salesmen of different kinds use. 'Free', for instance, is a popular word among both advertisers and politicians, although they use the word in different senses. Enough is generally known about the intended meaning to realize that they are using it in different senses, but in fact, the word is seldom defined in either context. It is emotive, not rational.

Working documents are usually written with little attempt to arouse emotion. The prevailing assumption is that if a document is a serious contribution to hard work it must be hard work to read. This belief doubtless accounts for the fact that most working documents are boring.

The use of exciting, provocative or emotive language in headings might, indeed, be counter-productive; but a responsible author will at least check that the emotions aroused by his words will help his audience to accept the message rather than prevent it from doing so.

One of the important factors in making documents attractive is novelty. A new layout, a new turn of phrase, a new colour on the cover may all help to make the reader think the document is lively. A shop which did not rearrange its windows regularly would soon lose custom. However, the writer should take care not to try to be too novel or emotive just for the sake of extra attention.

Is there such a thing as 'good English'?

The simple answer to this question is 'yes'. What is more important, and more difficult for most people to understand, is that good English is effective writing. If you can write so that the other person can understand it easily, the English is good, even though it is ungrammatical. This basic truth tends to be obscured in people's minds by the way they remember English being taught at school.

The result is that many people remember rules laid down in their early English classes for which no explanations were offered; and some continue in adult life to express horror when a newspaper headline or a BBC announcer breaks these remembered rules. It is most agreeable to feel superior to national institutions in this way, but if this attitude is carried over into the office it makes life unnecessarily difficult.

Commonly people believe either of two opposite extreme ideas: one that good English consists simply of arbitrary rules that have to be learnt; the other, that English is an art without rules and which cannot be learnt. Both these views are ridiculous.

The first view doubtless derives from learning to spell at school. A child entering the adult world needs to learn its ways, even without understanding them. The rules of spelling are tight, that is to say there is little disagreement between dictionaries on the conventional spelling; and most people find it helpful to have one spelling for words which they can then use with confidence. Moreover if spelling were not standardized, but based simply on pronunciation, it would remove one way of distinguishing between words of different meanings but the same pronunciation, such as 'their' and 'there'.

Unfortunately this leads to intolerance. Writers are forced to take into account readers who will be at least distracted by a word spelt in an unconventional way. So writers should conform to approved spellings, even though uniformity of spelling adds one extra task to the writer's load.

People who believe that spelling is either right or wrong, and believe the same about style, do not usually consult the authorities on style as frequently as they refer to a dictionary. Indeed if they did they would soon have to modify the view that it is all a question of rules to be learnt. For instance, the arrangement of words in a sentence, and the use of punctuation, is designed to make a document easy to read and difficult to misunderstand.

Good English consists simply of reasonable ways of writing. As a reasonable way may be different in different documents, good style cannot easily be summed up in a list of rules which can be applied uniformly. Fundamentally the writer has to work out what is the best way of expressing his message each time he writes.

The French have an Academie Française to give a quasi-legal standing to good French. The English-speaking nations have no such institution. Even correct spelling is only a consensus of agreement among educated people and is changing continuously. What was a mistake to the last generation may be fashionable today and the only correct method a generation from now. Fashion changes, sometimes for the better, sometimes for the worse. Those who believe that English consists in keeping to irrational rules will be likely to miss the point that what is traditional is not for that reason necessarily good. The argument 'we have always done it this way' is as bad in the realm of writing as anywhere else.

If a thing has always been done there is probably a good reason for it. But in that case do it because there is a good reason, not because it is traditional. Discover the reason if you can behind the tradition.

One of the fashions that has now virtually disappeared is that of referring to months as *inst, ult* and *prox*. This is a change for the better, and it is worth listing the reasons why this is a good change because these reasons provide the fundamental standards of good English and standards by which we should accept or reject school-made rules.

(a) The reader wants to know the month intended, and it is easiest to tell him directly. From the Latin abbreviation he has to identify the month intended by reference to the date on the document.

(b) Because the names of the months are understood by everybody, but Latin abbreviations by only a few.

(c) Because anything that looks like showing off is apt to irritate the reader. Latin or any other foreign language has this effect, particularly if there are good English equivalent words or phrases.

One of the most fundamental rules of common sense, which will distinguish between any alternative versions of the same thing, and be right at least nine times out of ten, is simply that shortest is best. Short words are better than long, short sentences are better than long sentences, a single word is better than a long phrase.

Learning how to write consists or should consist of seeing beyond the school-made rules to the principles of common sense which are fundamental. Given time it is not difficult to rewrite most business documents to make them more considerate, comprehensive, efficient and shorter.

It may, however, take a long time before you write automatically in the clearest and shortest way. Bad habits are difficult to dislodge and good habits difficult to acquire.

The 'pay-off' comes to the reader with the first good document you produce however long it may have taken to write. The 'pay-off' to the writer of learning how to think and write logically, will come only when he finds it quicker to write a good short letter than a bad long one. To achieve this without undue delay, constant practice and sensible supervision are necessary.

It is worth looking at Fowler's *Modern English Usage* to see how he deals with rules. Although he was a great scholar and is everywhere accepted as an authority, he does not state rules as though they were arbitrary. He gives the explanation. Look up his articles under 'Fetishes' and 'Superstitions', and you will find lists of the rules which he has rejected because he could find no reason for them. You may reject his views after having read the explanation, either because it does not seem convincing to you, or because it does not apply to your profession or occupation, or because you think the language has developed since the particular version (probably a revised one) that you are reading was written. That at least would be a more sensible attitude than not referring to Fowler because you regard your school memories as the ultimate arbiter.

Some people have a flair for detecting bad English. This is a definite gift like being good at spelling or having good taste in clothes. Those who are well on into adulthood and cannot spell or lack some artistic gift will be unlikely to change in these respects.

So while all writers should continue to think about and apply such common sense rules as 'shortest is best', there is more to presenting an effective document than that. Everyone has limitations and it is important to know what they are. Until they can change themselves they may have to rely on friends who can make good any deficiency.

In organizations where a document goes out in the name of the organization, it makes sense to use the skills of colleagues, whether in spelling or in achieving an elegant style. This will be taken up in the next two sections.

How to learn as you go along

Most people want to improve in their job. Writers are likely to learn automatically if they think about the subject, draft something one day and look at it the next. They also compare good and bad writing in their in-tray.

In an organization you can expect to learn from your superior. He may edit what you write, in which case you should have an editorial interview which is in effect private tuition in writing.

Create these opportunities if they do not occur; welcome them when they do. You will learn about many things, technical, administrative, political, as well as which writing is effective and which is not. You should also be able to discover some of the underlying reasons for failure.

Read books. Even if you are not already in the reading habit it makes sense to read any book which you find readable and is likely to be of use in your work. The books in the bibliography listed in appendix 4 will be a good start and they are all available in the public library. But report writers ought to have easy access to some of them at their place of work.

Learn by feedback. In the crudest sense this means that people will tell you when your writing is brilliant or terrible. The trouble here is that even assuming they are right, it it not easy either to repeat the brilliant or avoid the terrible. You can do this only if they tell you or you can work out for yourself the reasons for the brilliance or the awfulness.

But feedback is usually more subtle. You have to spot what is good and bad in your writing without people making it explicit. Editors frequently (but regrettably) rewrite a passage without it being obvious why the original would not serve; you have to ask them. Better feedback in many ways comes from the ultimate reader, the person in the other organization to whom your note or report is addressed. You should know whether he has responded favourably to your writing or not. It is worth analysing the result you have achieved, particularly if it is unsatisfactory. You may possibly come to the conclusion that your report would be rejected however you wrote it. But if you can establish the reasons which led to rejection, you can almost inevitably learn from them for the future.

It was Oscar Wilde in a cynical mood who said 'Experience is the name men give to their mistakes'; but in fact the most constructive thing to do with mistakes is analyse them and ensure that when you make mistakes in future they are different ones.

Feedback is so valuable that it may be unwise to leave it to chance; you will have to provoke it. Where the importance of the report justifies the time being spent, you should write two or more versions of a particular document or passage in a document. Then compare the versions. Sleep on the problem and compare the versions again next day. Get the views of other people, particularly those who know the readers better than you do. Nobody objects to their advice being asked and this free commodity is valuable even if in the particular instance you eventually decide to ignore it.

32

Do not be surprised if you find you prefer short versions to long. Shortest is best. It is as valuable to finish reading a document quickly as it is to do any other job quickly.

Be prepared for other factors in your analysis and do not ignore them because they are outside your control. The way a document is printed, the use of colour, the typeface and spacing, and even the design of the official letterhead, can all affect whether you find a document readable or not. Make a note of any ideas you have which require changes of policy. You may be unable to bring these changes about immediately, but if everybody ignored the questions of policy over which they seem to have no control, change would seldom come about at all.

Look at novels and newspapers that you may be reading and other examples of the work of professional writers. You may know that much of it will not apply to your own work, but it is likely that you can learn many lessons in studying the professionals closely.

Consider finally the value of courses. An intensive course in writing, with a mixture of practice and theory, can be a very good way of reminding you of, and consolidating, the basic principles of questioning your assumptions and of bringing a new approach to the writing part of your job. This may come from the staff guiding the course or from other course participants, or from simply having in a room a number of people concentrating for a longish period without interruption on this complex subject.

TABLES AND DIAGRAMS

The supposed Chinese proverb 'One picture is worth a thousand words' might sound like an artistic rather than a scientific statement: containing a grain of truth no doubt, but exaggerating it hopelessly for effect.

It would be as well to take it literally. If you do have to choose between expressing an idea in words or pictures, calculate the cost of production of each method of communication and the number of words that would be necessary to communicate a message that could be put across in a picture.

One thousand words is roughly 40 sentences. Whether it took 40 sentences to express the content of a picture, diagram, graph, or table, would depend on how much information the visual contained. It is a reasonable equation when you take into account that readers will make comparisons between many different pairs of items in a table, or between a string of numbers shown by a graph, to indicate a trend or possibly cause and effect.

If the 'picture' is at all complicated, it almost certainly takes longer to produce than a thousand words. Secretaries can take down a thousand words of dictation in 10 minutes and type them in 15 to 20 minutes. It would probably take longer than that to produce a rough draft of a graph or table and the time taken to lay it out

Figure 1
People in households: by type of household and family in which they live, 1979

Great Britain

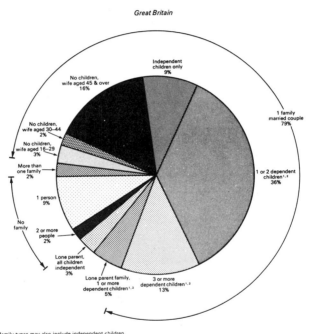

¹ These family types may also include independent children.
² Dependent children are those aged 0–15, plus those aged 16–18 in full-time education.

Source: General Household Survey, 1979

precisely is usually much longer. It is the cost of production which explains why most books have no pictures. But the overwhelming reason why one picture is in fact worth more than a thousand words is that it is less of an intellectual strain. It is more fun. If a

34

page of a report is a mixture of picture and prose, it is the picture that first attracts attention.

The reasons for this well known phenomenon are not clear. However, it seems to be another aspect of the truth that concrete nouns, that is nouns that can be pictured by the imagination, are much more readily understood than abstract nouns and that the good public speaker uses visual aids. You might think that this was simply because visual aids were pictures; but even if the speaker writes words on the blackboard or projects them onto a screen, the message is easier to assimilate than if he simply spoke.

Figure 2
Young people in the education system: by age and stage of education at January 1979

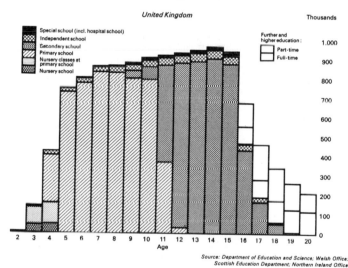

Source: Department of Education and Science; Welsh Office;
Scottish Education Department; Northern Ireland Office

Source: *Social Trends 11*. HMSO, London, 1980.

'Yes, I see' is an expression meaning 'Yes, I understand'. It seems to have a literal significance: the more that you can actually see the easier it is to understand.

The figures shown on pages 34–39 give examples of various ways of presenting information pictorially.

A pie chart (*see* figure 1 on page 34) is useful for comparing the different slices of the pie. It depends on having one total which can be divided into component parts.

A histogram (*see* figure 2 on page 35) consists of a series of bars each of which can be divided like the pie chart, but taken together show trends over time, and make it easier to compare the rise or decline of one component from bar to bar.

A more sophisticated bar chart (*see* figure 3, below) can be made by putting the zero line in the middle rather than at the bottom. In effect this is like two plain bar charts one underneath the other, the lower one upside down.

Figure 3
Average taxes paid and benefits received: by household type, 1978

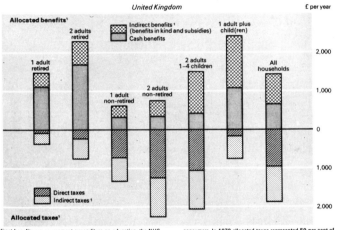

¹ Indirect benefits are government expenditure on education, the NHS and welfare foods, plus subsidies on housing, food, and rail travel. Indirect taxes are mainly rates, VAT and various duties, but they also include some taxes paid by industry and passed onto consumers. In 1978 allocated taxes represented 59 per cent of government income, and allocated benefits represented 47 per cent of government expenditure.

Source: Central Statistical Office

Source: Social Trends 11. HMSO, London, 1980.

A graph (*see* figure 4 on page 37) is widely used and commonly understood. It is in effect a smoothed-out version of the histogram. Graphs are more appropriate for units where you may need the figure at any point on the line. For instance the number of people employed in any industry is not greatly different from one day to the next and the figures for 1978 will be probably somewhere between those for 1977 and 1979. The numbers employed in March of any year will be somewhere between those employed in February and those employed in April. But in many statistical presentations this does not apply. The annual profits of a company can be reached by adding up the profits obtained during the year. There is no significance in any points on the line except for the

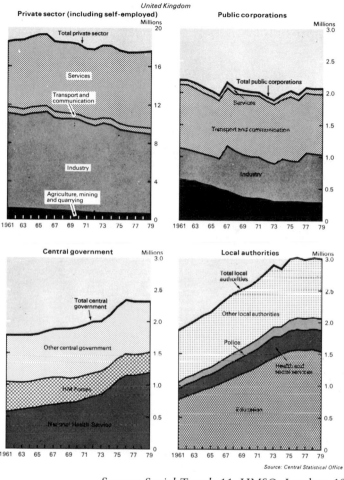

Figure 4
People in employment: by sector and industry

United Kingdom

Private sector (including self-employed)

Public corporations

Central government

Local authorities

Source: Central Statistical Office

Source: Social Trends 11. HMSO, London, 1980.

annual totals. For this kind of statistic therefore a histogram is clearer and more appropriate.

A bar chart enables the imagination to grasp the difference in size between different parts of a total, rather as the pie chart does. A histogram has some of the advantages of a graph. Approximate comparisons between one year and another, as well as trends, can be rapidly spotted.

The imaginative use of bar charts, and indeed of all pictorial presentations, enables report writers to use them to express quite complicated ideas.

Flow charts (*see* figure 5 below), sometimes called algorithms, are another invaluable way of simplifying the complicated.

Figure 5
The flow of household incomes, taxes, and benefits

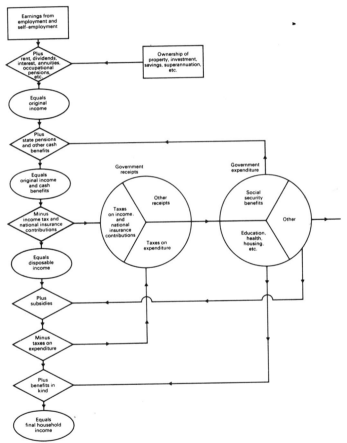

Source: *Social Trends 11*. HMSO, London, 1980.

They have been used in work study as a means of identifying the stages in a given production process, because they help enormously to see how the process could be improved. They have been

38

Figure 6
Sample: report production flow chart

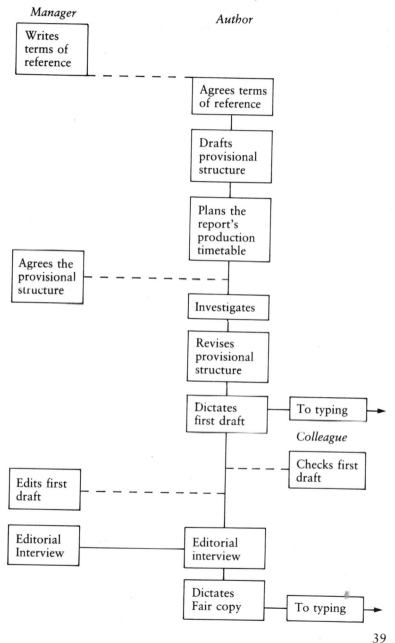

increasing in popularity for such purposes as describing which individuals are entitled to what social security benefits, because they convey the message more rapidly than sentences. The reader can skip those parts of the diagram with which he is not concerned; ambiguity is more obvious and hence can be avoided in constructing the flow chart; and the writer does not have to worry about the finer points of grammar. They do, however, take time and expertise to draw.

If it is not clear what decisions your readers are going to take on the basis of the diagram, it is difficult to produce a good one. If, however, you are clear about their objectives this will help you choose a pictorial method and if necessary invent your own.

Figure 6 on page 39 gives a flow chart showing a possible sequence of events in the production of a long report.

6

The value of editing

Almost every piece of writing can be improved after a second read. The author of a report naturally rereads his draft, perhaps many times over. Each time he is likely to find a word, a sentence, a paragraph or even a page that can be more succinctly or accurately expressed. This is the first stage of the editorial process. The following chapter is not so much about that initial stage, the author's editing, but the stage that follows, when another person sees the draft and comments on its effectiveness.

Virtually all written material, whether it is managerial, technical, fiction, a film script or publicity material, benefits from the 'second eye'. As a result of another person seeing a draft, any need for changes and improvements, either minor or major, can be identified and the desired alterations recommended. This is the second stage of the editorial process. In organizations and certainly in public bodies major reports go through the editorial process before they are released to the readers. Of course, there may be no need for further refinements after the author has completed his editing.

The necessity for editing in large organizations arises from the nature of the job and the allocation of responsibility. The senior civil servant, borough treasurer, or partner in the firm, has to be responsible for any statement made by his part of the organization. Subordinate staff deal with all the minor details and draft the report; superiors check it and authorize publication.

The value of this, as of any other form of delegation, is plain. But there is a special value in report editing. An author cannot always adequately judge his own work; it needs another angle. The writer is often too close to the investigation he reports and to the words he uses in his report, to judge its impact on the readers. Sometimes he has re-read his draft so often he can no longer see the wood for the trees. A second read is vital in spotting ambiguity. It can and should

41

be done by an equal, because equals are less inhibited in giving and taking criticism than manager and subordinate. But if the senior manager has to edit the report anyway because it is his responsibility, he will provide another angle on the ambiguities too.

In many organizations the procedure is laid down by the employer. Frequently the author's name on the report is the person who first drafted it. In the civil service and in most businesses, the seniority of the author depends on the importance of the message. Some organizations try to delegate the drafting as far down as possible, while pushing the responsibility for final authorization as high up as possible. There are then layers of editors in the middle, trying to modify what someone below them has written to make it acceptable to the editor next up the line. This is time-wasting.

Editors are clearly essential and useful. Since reports are written for employers and superiors the best motivation to good report writing will come from constructive editing. No matter how good report writers are, if the editing is poor the finished article will be poor.

THE ROLE OF THE EDITOR

Every document has to be edited. But this section is not concerned with editing which the original author should do automatically with any document of any importance. It is concerned primarily with the editor who is the writer's manager.

In some organizations, particularly research organizations, there is an editor who has a staff relationship with the writer. His job is to comment on all documents produced by the organization, but only about their structure and style, not their technical content of which he may be presumed to be less well informed than either the writer or the writer's bosses.

The fact that he deals with all reports means that he can become a specialist in matters of structure and style and thus an acceptable referee in the event of an otherwise unproductive conflict of view on these subjects between the writer and his boss. Papers for publication in professional journals can be vetted to see that they meet the requirements of the editor of the journal concerned; and often enough the specialist staff editor can recommend the most appropriate journal for publication. If the organization has a document outlining house style he can see that it is followed.

The only difficulty with this kind of editor is the same that arises in all divisions of responsibility between staff and line. There is a difficulty in describing the limits of the authority of each. Too often in practice the staff editor is only advisory and line managers with a strong point of view on style or structure are reluctant to accept his advice. Editing may then include an element of negotiation.

In any event, there are important matters about a good report which can be adequately assessed only by the line manager, such as the technical content, what is relevant for the purpose and readers and what matter is politically sensitive. Therefore all organizations should take the line manager's editing seriously and in most organizations he will be the only one responsible.

Where the editor is the line manager, his role varies according to who commissioned the report in the first place; himself, a higher authority inside the organization, or someone such as a client outside the organization.

Where the editor also commissioned the report in the first place, he has two jobs to do, which may be difficult to separate. He has to digest it as a basis for his own action, and he has to comment on the way it was written as part of his duty to train his subordinate to write reports. It is a pity that the first job is likely to crowd out the second, as this is an ideal opportunity (the editor being the ultimate reader) to develop the author's report writing skills.

Where the report originates from an authority higher than the editor, such as a board of directors, and it is addressed to them, he does not have to take action; but he has to modify the report if necessary so that it does not discredit himself and his unit. Ideally the modifications should be opportunities for the author to develop his skill.

Too often there is no time for the editor to point out what passages need modification and why, and leave it to the author to rewrite the passages to meet the editor's criticism. If a deadline is to be met, the editor has to rewrite it himself.

If the modifications are never explained, this leaves the author no wiser, because he does not know why the original was not acceptable, and if he has put considerable work into his version it will leave him very frustrated.

Where the report is for a client, it is one degree more remote. The editor is putting the document into suitable form for the board of directors, the intermediate readers, so they can present it to the client or ultimate readers and get it accepted. This is another instance where it may be easier in the short run to rewrite offending passages rather than to explain the complexities of interacting personalities and motives which may justify some changes that he makes.

All editors should aim at not editing the document at all. Therefore the editor should monitor the amount of editing that he has to do and if his training is effective it will lessen with each report from a particular author. If the editor is rewriting 50 per cent of the report, there must be a very expensive weakness in the system. Few editors in fact wish to rewrite more than they have to. Yet in many organizations, those who write reports imagine that the editor grasps a blue pencil before reading and intends to use it as much as possible.

This would be futile, not so much because it would create unnecessary work, although that objection is serious enough, but for the suffering it would cause the original author, as he saw his 'baby' pulled and pushed beyond recognition.

Commonly he suffers in silence. It is not in his interests to criticize his manager's decisions. And to question the reasons for editorial changes, even though he simply wanted to learn from the editor, would be taken as a criticism. The more unjustifiable he thinks the changes are, the more likely that any attempt to elicit an explanation would lead to conflict and therefore the less likely he is to ask. Most managers do not create the time to discuss their changes with the subordinates that they should.

To avoid the demoralizing effect that this lack of communication has, editors should discuss any corrections they have to make with the writer. If there is a deadline to meet and the corrections cannot be discussed before the report is issued, then the discussion should take place later. Ideally, the editor should not rewrite himself, but indicate what is the objection to any particular passage and obtain the author's rewording of the passage.

This ensures that the editor amends passages only where he is convinced that there is a genuine mistake; it ensures that the author can learn from his mistakes; it enables the editor to check, by seeing the author's rewritten version, that the lesson has been understood; and it should take up less of the editor's valuable time than rewriting it himself.

There are four aspects of the line manager's job that are relevant to his editorial role: he has authority to decide what goes in; power to advance or hinder the subordinate's progress; he is busy; and he has a duty to train his subordinates.

His authority to be the final arbiter on the wording of even trivial passages is seldom questioned. Even in research organizations, where a report is going out in the name of the first author and only incidentally of the organization, a line manager can usually impose his will and his words on those of the named author. This not only has a bad effect on the author's morale, but is likely to result in writing which is a mixture of styles. The editor does this not by right but by using his power as a line manager.

The editor's power, in his capacity as a boss, is given to him by the employer. It usually includes an element of the ability to hire and fire, the power to recommend for promotion and the power to allocate duties so as to make the life of any particular subordinate easy or disagreeable. This power entails a corresponding responsibility to those over whom it is exercised. A manager's job is not only to achieve his own objectives or the objectives of the team; he has to find out what individuals want to get out of their work and if possible arrange that they shall.

Editors tend to be busy people. They can only get through their work by arranging it in some order of priority. Producing a well-written document before a deadline is often the top priority, but coaching subordinates by going through the document and seeing if they can grasp what was wrong with the original version, is usually given a low priority.

This leads to the paradox, similar to that affecting delegation and all other systems for saving the time of senior managers, that those who have the most to gain cannot afford the initial investment. Even if you know that half an hour's constructive discussion with a subordinate would save five hours of his time and five hours of yours when he next writes a report, that knowledge does not provide the half an hour necessary to turn the vicious spiral into a virtuous one.

All managers have a responsibility to train their subordinates. It is possible and desirable to meet this responsibility in part by sending subordinates on courses, including courses in writing reports. However, it is unlikely that the course will achieve much unless the line manager has been monitoring the author's progress before the course. If he has identified specifically the training objectives which the author should have for his course (and discussed them with the author) the course is likely to be fruitful. Moreover if the editor monitors the author's progress after the course he can identify its influence.

It happens too often, however, that he sends the author on a course because he has too little time or perhaps too little confidence to coach him individually and regards the course as a substitute. This may well have the undesirable consequence of making the vicious spiral worse. After the course the author may well feel able to write better than his boss and his irritation at seeing his work altered without having the opportunity to discuss the changes will only increase.

Much conflict and inefficiency will disappear if author and editor work together at several stages (*see* figure 6 on page 39):

(a) Ideally the editor should write out the terms of reference and give them to the author, allowing opportunity for discussion before he starts. These should include the purpose of the report, the intended readers, the scope and limits of the report, any authority to use special resources or money, the time allowed for its completion and whether it is to be confidential and to whom. Where this does not and perhaps cannot happen, the author should write his own terms of reference and give a copy to his editor, so that if he is working on the wrong lines he can be corrected before much time is wasted. They should be discussed and any other matter which the author should know before he starts can be communicated face to face.

(b) Editor and author may agree the structure of the report, that is the list of headings and subheadings, before writing the text. A short discussion at this stage, particularly with those learning the art of writing reports in a new environment, will save long hours of editorial time subsequently.

(c) The editor will usually have two parts to his work: to read the report by himself, making notes (preferably on a separate sheet) and then an interview with the author to discuss the points raised. Such an editing interview has three aims for the editor who is also a line manager. First it will improve this particular document. Secondly it will help to train and motivate the author. Thirdly it will check that the author is receiving enough support from other parts of the organization, including guidance on what standards the organization expects, enough time for writing, a suitable place, and proper clerical support.

The editing interview will then be concerned with meeting these aims and, in particular where a part has to be rewritten, with explaining the reasons for it to the writer and asking him to rewrite it. Some organizations are doing this effectively already.

Appendix 1: shorter reports

Letters and memoranda

The dividing line between reports, letters and memoranda (memos) is not rigid; reports can overlap with letters and memos. The definition of reports at the beginning of chapter 1 could cover letters and memos too. Conventionally a letter begins 'Dear . . .' and ends 'Yours . . .'. A memo is an internal letter, that is, a letter addressed to someone serving the same employer and normally headed 'Memorandum', but lacking the 'Dear . . .' and the 'Yours . . .'. A report has a structure such as that described in chapter 4, but letters and memos do not usually have so detailed a structure unless they are also reports.

It is often useful to present a report as a letter, particularly if it is from a professional person to a private client. Letters beginning 'Dear' and a name seem less official and more friendly to most people. Nevertheless, when both author and reader are within one organization, reports and memos usually replace letters.

If a report is to be sent to another organization, it is best written as described in chapter 4 with a covering letter. This covering letter can mention points in the report which the reader may find particularly important, or points additional to those in the report suitable only for the reader of the covering letter.

Short reports in letter or memo form can be divided into two sections, the facts and the action. These may be two sentences or two paragraphs or, in a longer report, two groups of headings, for instance:

FACTS — known and agreed
— new and acceptable to both writer and reader
— new and require action

ACTION — already taken
— which I propose to take
— which I recommend the reader to take

If the report is so long that this structure will not be adequate, then it is best to develop a structure closer to that described in chapter 4.

AGENDAS AND MINUTES

An agenda is a list of items to be discussed during a meeting and is drawn up in advance of the meeting. The minutes are drawn up after the meeting and are a record of what took place at the meeting.

The basic purpose of each is clear. The agenda helps those attending to prepare for the meeting and control or contribute to the discussion. The minutes help ensure that matters discussed and decisions agreed are faithfully recorded and implemented. But the purposes may go wider than this, and vary according to the kind of meeting. There are three main kinds, autocratic, democratic and advisory. As they are often confused, and the confusion wastes time, it is worth explaining them here.

(a) Autocratic

This is the normal type of meeting in a business, when an executive summons his subordinates to discuss some problem. The meeting, and the supporting papers including agenda and minutes if any, have no ultimate purpose except that in the mind of the executive. The executive may not devise a list of items for discussion until the meeting has assembled, so that those attending do not know what it will be about until they arrive. He may not wish to keep any record of what happened. Alternatively he may write a memorandum after the meeting is over, giving a skeleton account of what happened and the decisions he has taken as a result of the meeting. On the other hand if he wants those present to think about the subjects beforehand he must send them some indication in advance. And if he wants to refer to the meeting after some months, or in a discussion at a more senior level, he will need a list of decisions taken and probably also the arguments leading to those decisions. It is in any event being done for his benefit and so he must decide what is required.

(b) Democratic

At this kind of meeting those attending have been elected according

48

to some constitution; decisions are taken by vote, at least in the last resort; and the chairman and secretary are there to help members reach a decision, rather than the members being there to help the chairman as in the autocratic meeting. Agendas exist to ensure that elected members receive proper and constitutional notice of the meeting, and minutes, so that the body that elected the meeting (for instance, the annual general meeting that elects a committee to run a club) have direct or indirect knowledge of what the elected members have been doing.

Minutes have therefore to be written impartially, by a secretary who is himself elected according to the constitution, and should be signed by the chairman (also elected) as correct at the following meeting, after members have had an opportunity to comment on them and correct them if necessary.

(c) Advisory

By definition an advisory meeting does not take a decision. There is therefore no voting and no precise accountability to a superior body, though the superior body or bodies appoint them and expect them to sift the evidence and write a report. The people appointed to take part in an advisory meeting often represent different groups, perhaps with conflicting interests or views, and discussion consists largely in an attempt to reach a consensus of agreement. When the meeting is not unanimous, there may be two or more incompatible opinions or ideas offered. Those who read the report will usually want to know the views of minorities as well as of the majority.

The distinction between the kinds of meeting may be blurred when there is a combination of people from different traditions; notably when managers, accustomed to executive and autocratic meetings, swift decisions, and leadership from the chair, are sitting round the table with trade unionists, accustomed to reaching slow democratic decisions in a formal and constitutional framework. The successful committee member must understand both traditions, know which applies in any given meeting, and make allowances for those from a different tradition.

If the advisory meeting is 'one-off' the minutes become the report and will include the advice given. However, a body meeting several times for advisory purposes, such as a Royal Commission, will only issue a report at the end of the series of meetings. Minutes of the meetings will have little purpose outside the meetings themselves.

They will simply help members to crystallize their thoughts for the next meeting, and serve as raw material for the final report.

In democratic and advisory meetings the paperwork helps to plan the meetings and helps members to know what has been decided and (usually) why. It has another purpose in democratic meetings: it can help the people who have elected the members of the meeting to know how their representatives have done their duties. In this *Hansard* serves a similar purpose in telling members of the public about the House of Commons. Agendas and minutes are always useful for absentees, and minutes may be useful for posterity. For instance, a club that wishes to hold a Christmas function will find it helpful to refer to the minutes of meetings arranging corresponding functions for the two or three previous years.

These various readers and their purposes will affect what is relevant for minutes and agendas.

A full agenda looks something like this:

The third meeting of the Wellingford Tennis Club Committee.
To be held on (*date*) at (*time*) at (*place*).

AGENDA
1 Welcome and apologies for absence
2 Minutes of the last meeting (*date*)
3 Matters arising from the minutes
4 Correspondence (or, Secretary's report)
5 Treasurer's report
6⎫
7⎬ (*Items of business as required*)
8⎭
9 Any other business (*or, AOB*)
10 Date, time, and place of next meeting.
L.P. Green (Hon. Sec.)
(*date of issuing agenda.*)
(*possibly list of members to be circulated.*)

If the agenda item has a supporting paper, it is usually numbered and described as follows, or in some similar way:

6 *Forthcoming Events. See Note 4, report of the Functions subcommittee.*
And then Note 4 will be attached, with all the other supporting

papers, behind the agenda. The number of the note will not necessarily coincide with the number of the item of the agenda, and some items may have more than one supporting note.

Supporting notes may be either copies of documentary evidence or fully argued cases. Documentary evidence might be something like the application forms, if the meeting had to make a short list for an appointment, or plans, if the meeting had to authorize expenditure on a building. Argued cases would be something like a small report giving the committee the reasons for a course of action. The structure of the argued case deserves thought. It is usually best to start with the recommendation here, because most members of meetings will be interested in that first. The structure in full might go as follows:

1 Recommendation
2 History of the problem
3 All available options now (including the option of doing nothing)
4 Arguments against each of the non-selected options
5 Objections to the course of action recommended
6 Answers to these objections
7 Full implications of accepting the recommendation.

Minutes may be headed 'Minutes of the third meeting of the Wellingford Tennis Club Committee on (date)'.

There should follow a list of those present, indicating who was chairman and secretary and any other significant officers. After that the numbering of the minutes should follow the numbering of the items on the agenda. Thus item 1 will record apologies for absence, and item 2 any amendments to the minutes of the last meeting made before they were accepted as a correct record.

The nature of the meeting will determine how full the minutes should be. It is always necessary to record decisions, and who is responsible for carrying them out (some minutes have a special column headed 'Action' giving the names or initials of those responsible, so that members can quickly remind themselves of their own duties). But it is not always necessary to put in the minutes all the points which led up to the decision, and the secretary must decide this according to who is reading the minutes and for what purpose.

Minutes are usually written in indirect speech. This means reported speech one tense further into the past without quotation marks. Hence where Mr Gusset says 'We are making slow progress', the minutes would read: 'Mr Gusset said that they were making slow progress'. It is written throughout in the third person (he, she, it, they, etc, instead of I, we, or you) and is more remote in tense, time and place.

A REPORT OF A MEETING

Those who appoint representatives to a meeting may well require them to write a report on it. Sometimes the representative can simply send his copy of the minutes, but often the minutes are not available in time, or they are full of irrelevant matter, have too little of the representative's views and nothing of his helpful explanations. So the representative has to produce his own report of the meeting.

There is a great difference between the minutes of a meeting and a report of the same meeting. There can be only one official set of minutes, but there can be as many reports of a meeting as people attending. Indeed one person can write several different reports on the meeting for different purposes. Minutes have to be impartial, to serve the purposes of all and to be read by any one, but a report of a meeting may be written selectively for one purpose and one reader. They are also different in form. The form of the minutes is the special form just described, whereas a report of a meeting could be in memo form, if short, or in the full report form described in chapter 4.

Appendix 2: grammar

USE OF GRAMMAR

In any specialist subject it is necessary to have names for the various parts of that subject, or any objects within it, which need analysis. It is easier to discuss the subject when something has gone wrong, for instance with a car, if those discussing it use the correct technical terms for the component parts. Grammar consists of the technical terms involved in analysing a piece of writing, and the proper use of these technical terms in identifying and correcting faults.

This section contains enough grammar to enable the ordinary working writer to analyse his writing and if necessary improve it.

WORDS AND PARTS OF SPEECH

Noun   A noun is a word used as the name of a person or thing. Examples are: Tom, butter, circle and justice.

The name of a specific person or organization, and sometimes of a specific abstract idea, is called a proper noun and usually has an initial capital letter. Examples: Tom, the Foreign Office, Symphony.

An abstract noun is one invented by a mind to describe the real world outside. You cannot draw or photograph the thing which an abstract noun represents. Examples of abstract nouns are: justice, love, information, confidence.

Pronoun   Pronouns behave like nouns, but they are not the name itself. The person or thing they refer to can be discovered only from the context or custom. Examples are: we, your, it, theirs, who, that.

Verb   A verb is a word which says what a noun is doing or that the noun exists. Examples: run, hit, buy, come, am, have, would be.

Verbs can vary in Number, Tense, Mood and Voice.

Variation in number is simply between singular and plural: I am, but we are; he has, but they have.

Tense refers to the time during which the action takes place. The basic tenses are past, present and future, but there are many variations on these, mostly formed by using two or more verbs together. Thus the present includes 'I run' and 'I am running'.

The moods of a verb are indicative, subjunctive, imperative and infinitive. The indicative is the normal form. It includes past, present, future, and all the time variants. The subjunctive is a mood to denote something thought rather than actual, and used to express a wish or command, or a conditional event. It is declining in use; but it remains in such common expressions as 'if I *were* you' (not was or am or will be) and 'I move that the resolution *be* accepted'.

The imperative is for giving instructions, and is used in recipes and manuals. Examples: Take 4 ozs of sugar. Do not park on the double yellow lines. Keep smiling. The imperative verbs in these sentences are 'take', 'park' and 'keep'. It is much the clearest and shortest way of giving any instruction.

The voice of a verb refers to whether the noun is at the giving or the receiving end of the action. 'The man kicks the bull', gives the active 'kicks'; the 'bull was kicked by the man' gives the passive 'was kicked'. Similarly:

Active	Passive
He will eat the food.	The food will be eaten by him.
Have received.	Have been received.
Will buy.	Will be bought.

Note that the supporting verbs 'will' and 'have' do not make the verb passive; only some part of the verb 'to be'. The active is shorter and more logical than the passive, and is normally preferable.

The infinitive is a form of the verb which serves as a noun. It begins with the word 'to'. Thus: to hit, to run, to come, to buy.

The past infinitive is made by taking the infinitive of the verb 'to have' and following it with the past participle of the verb concerned, thus: to have hit, to have bought. The future infinitive is neither so common nor so fixed as the past. It might be 'to be about to hit' or 'to be going to buy'.

A 'split infinitive' is an infinitive as described, with another word immediately after the 'to' and before any verb. 'To wisely buy' is a split infinitive, and so is 'to wisely have bought', but not 'to have wisely bought' because the infinitive 'to have' remains uninterrupted. Unfortunately many people imagine (wrongly) that a split infinitive is always wrong. To avoid giving offence therefore, it is worth trying to avoid splitting the infinitive. This may, however, lead to ambiguity, which is likely to be worse than giving offence. If you can think of a way of avoiding splitting the infinitive without being ambiguous, this is the ideal solution for most working writers.

Verbs are called transitive or intransitive. A transitive verb is a word like 'kick' or 'carry', which makes no sense without a noun afterwards, known as its object. An intransitive verb, like 'come' or 'live', cannot have an object immediately following, but may have an indirect object, that is an object preceded by a preposition. You may live, or you may live *for* money, but you do not live money. You may come, or you may come *to* me, but you do not come me.

Adjective A word which describes a noun is an adjective. Examples: lively, second, English.

In technical matters it is becoming increasingly common to use nouns as adjectives. Though this is unfortunate in principle, because it can lead to ambiguity, it seems inevitable. Our need to use nouns as adjectives is spreading more rapidly than our ability to invent suitable adjectival forms of the noun. Thus we might talk about 'the recruitment advertising growth rate', in which the three middle words are nouns being used as adjectives.

When a verb is to be used as an adjective, it is called a participle. The present participle ends -ing, as in 'the running man', 'the goods coming by rail'. The past participle usually ends -ed, as in 'the service provided includes', 'the facts discussed'. Some verbs do not have the -ed ending, and the past participle is some equivalent, as in 'the meeting held on' (not 'holded'); or 'the work undertaken' (not 'undertooked'). There is no future participle.

Article The words 'a' and 'an' are called indefinite articles, and 'the' is the definite article. They are a special kind of adjective.

Adverb The simplest way to explain an adverb is that it is any word which describes something else but is not an adjective. It may describe a verb, as 'quickly' in 'he ran quickly'; it may describe an adjective, as in 'the obviously premature suggestion', where 'premature' is the adjective describing 'suggestion', and 'obviously' is the adverb describing 'premature'. It may describe another adverb, as in 'not easily deceived', where 'not' is an adverb describing the other adverb 'easily' which describes the adjective 'deceived'; or 'arrived unexpectedly soon' where 'arrived' is a verb, described by the adverb 'soon', which is described by the other adverb 'unexpectedly'.

Sometimes an adverb is more properly said to describe a group of words than one other single word. In 'we will reduce costs, however difficult it may be' 'however' describes the adjective 'difficult'. But in 'we have reduced costs; it was, however, difficult', 'however' describes the clause 'it was difficult'. Many other adverbs act in this way: moreover, nevertheless, therefore and meanwhile. Because they describe a clause or sentence by indicating the way it is related to another clause or sentence, they are often confused with conjunctions.

The chief fault that results from confusing these adverbs with conjunctions is in joining together into one sentence two groups of words each of which makes sense independently. The reader must be told somehow that they are independent groups of words. This may be done either by using a full stop to indicate that they are separate sentences, or by a semi-colon, or by a conjunction which indicates the necessary break. Thus you may say:

We have reduced costs. It was difficult.
or: We have reduced costs; it was difficult.
or: We have reduced costs, but it was difficult.

It is not grammatically correct, and may mislead the reader, to join these two independent clauses with neither a strong punctuation mark nor conjunction. Thus the following three versions would all be ungrammatical:

We have reduced costs it was difficult.
We have reduced costs, it was difficult.
We have reduced costs, however it was difficult.

To avoid this mistake it is not necessary to know whether the words you are using are adverbs or conjunctions, and in fact few people do know this. Nor does it help much to use a dictionary, because some of the words concerned are adverbs and conjunctions at different times. There is a simple test. A conjunction does not belong to either of the two groups of words which it joins. There is only one place, therefore, that it can be put, which is outside both the groups. You cannot shift 'and' or 'but' in any sentence without making nonsense (or quite a different sense). But an adverb belongs to one of the groups concerned, and may come in several places. For instance, 'however' may come as the first, the second, or the last word in the phrase to which it is attached, and often in other places as well, without changing the meaning. When it comes between two independent clauses, it might belong to either, causing ambiguity, unless there were a semi-colon or a conjunction to indicate the end of one clause and the beginning of the next.

Conjunctions These are often called joining words, but as the adverbs described above are also in a sense joining words, it would perhaps be better to describe conjunctions as separating words. The test just described, that if a word linking or separating two groups of words cannot be moved from its position, it is a conjunction, will serve to identify them. In fact there are not many in common use; the usual ones are: although, and, because, but, for, if, nor, or, so, unless, until, while. All these may join clauses, and some of them can join nouns ('fish and chips'), verbs ('walk or run'), adjectives ('strong but light'), and adverbs ('quickly and quietly').

Conjunctions, like adverbs, may quite lawfully come at the beginning of a sentence, to indicate the connection with the previous sentence. It is not necessarily wrong to begin a sentence with 'and' or 'but'. It can be rather unoriginal to begin every sentence this way, which is no doubt why children are taught not to do so, but it is never grammatically wrong and it can be effective.

Prepositions These are short words indicating, as the term 'preposition' partly implies, the position of one thing compared to another. Examples include: in, under, over, by, with, from, to, for, out, of, from, upon.

To make sense, these words usually have to be followed by nouns, and there is a tradition that they ought always to be so followed, or in other words that it is wrong to end a sentence with a preposition. This view is hardly tenable today. Many verbs change their meaning slightly or even seriously by the addition of a preposition afterwards: to go out, to run in. Likewise adjectives: full up, worn out.

Another reason why the convention is dying is that a sentence or clause ending with a preposition may be much more telling than one where that sequence of words is avoided. It was Churchill's contribution to changing this so-called rule, to say of it 'this is the kind of nonsense up with which I will not put'. That is more striking than 'I will not put up with this kind of nonsense'. Feel free to put a preposition at the end of a clause or a sentence if that will convey the message better.

Interjection This is the prevailing term in grammar for a word which expresses emotion rather than a thought or sentence: help! well! It is common enough in conversation and novels but has little part in reports; but see 'Exclamation mark' below, on page 63.

PHRASES

A phrase, defined grammatically, is a group of words making sense together, but lacking a verb, and therefore not complete independent sense. For example, the phrase 'by the way' is common and as far as it goes makes sense. But it implies that there is something more to come, or else that there was something before it began.

Phrases may take on the role of one of the other parts of speech in a given sentence. The examples chosen are simply to illustrate the grammatical point, and are too close to cliché to be usable.

A noun phrase might be 'the sands of time' or 'the back of beyond'.

Examples of adjectival phrases would include 'under consideration' and 'with great prospects'.

Adverbial phrases would include 'in confidence' and 'by first class mail'.

A phrase may do the work of a verb, and so be a verb phrase, as long as it does not make complete sense. This means either that the verb is in the infinitive, or that the phrase does not include a noun which, to make sense, it plainly needs. Thus verb phrases include, using the infinitive, 'to save our bacon' or 'to whet the appetite'. Or a verb phrase might take a form like 'opened an account' or 'reserved judgement'.

CLAUSES

A clause is a group of words together not only making sense, like a phrase, but making complete sense; capable if necessary of standing as a complete independent sentence. This means it must have not only a noun as the subject of the verb, but also a finite verb. The meaning of the word 'finite' here is that it has to be a verb acting as a verb, not a verbal noun like an infinitive, nor a verbal adjective like a participle. Thus 'going away' is not a proper clause, because 'going' is a participle and not a finite verb, and there is no subject. But 'I am going away' is a clause, because the noun 'I' is the subject and the finite verb 'am' follows it.

The well known phrase which so often, alas, finishes letters, 'assuring you of our best attention at all times', is thus not a clause and cannot be a sentence by itself. The same objection applies to an opening sentence like 'referring to your letter of 10th May'. If the sentence does not indicate who is assuring or referring, then

58

'assuring' and 'referring' are called unattached participles or hanging participles, and are grammatical errors.

Like a phrase, a clause may serve instead of a part of speech. Consider this sentence:

> That local authorities would lose power from the policy that the Government was advocating became obvious as the months passed.

The clause 'that local authorities would lose power' is a substitute for a noun. If you substitute for that phrase 'the dishonour', you change the sense but not the grammatical structure or correctness.

The clause 'that the Government was advocating' is an adjectival clause, describing 'policy'. It could be replaced by the adjective 'official', but that word would have to go before 'policy'.

The clause 'as the months passed' is adverbial, describing the verb 'became'. It could be replaced by 'quickly'.

To emphasize the distinction between clauses and phrases, in each of these clauses there is a noun: respectively, 'authorities', 'Government' and 'months'. There are also verbs: respectively, 'lose', 'was advocating' and 'passed'. There is also an introductory word before each clause joining it on to the sentence: respectively, 'that', 'that' and 'as'. These linking words are not always essential, and in this sentence the second 'that' is not necessary.

SENTENCES

This word is popularly used to mean the part of a written composition which goes from one full stop to the next. Writing a grammatical sentence is not difficult providing the writer thinks of the full stop as being an opportunity for the reader to clear his memory of the words in the sentence just concluded. Until he reaches the full stop he may have to keep the words in his short-term memory, which is a strain if the sentence is long and badly constructed. If it is ungrammatical he may never discover the meaning.

A formal sentence should consist of at least a subject and a verb, but need contain no more, so that 'prices rose' is a grammatical sentence. Two such clauses, sometimes called main clauses, can be joined by a conjunction to form a sentence. For example: 'prices rose although interest rates were high'. 'Although' is the conjunction and the words following form an independent clause. A

59

sentence with two clauses joined by a conjunction is sometimes called a compound sentence. A sentence including a subordinate clause, such as an adjectival or adverbial clause, is sometimes called a complex sentence. To the basic sentence 'prices rose' we could add an adjectival clause thus:

Prices, which the Government had expected to fall, rose.

It is possible to make long sentences by adding on adjectival or adverbial clauses with the appropriate linking words, and by adding other main clauses with appropriate conjunctions. However, even a four-clause sentence can be difficult to construct, and the reader may well find a longer sentence difficult to follow even if it is constructed correctly and grammatically.

Punctuation

Full stop

This says to the reader 'we have now finished a grammatically self-contained group of words. If you have understood the message, you can forget the words used to convey it'. As full stops are only used at the end of sentences, this statement gives sufficient guidance on the use of full stops.

Full stops are, however, used sometimes for abbreviations; as long as a writer is consistent, and follows a house style if there is one, this should present no difficulty.

Colon

This sign, :, is now chiefly used to indicate that the list of items, which the words before the colon have led the reader to expect, will come immediately after the colon. Although many people use a dash after the colon (:—) the dash is always unnecessary and widely believed to be incorrect.

A colon serves like other punctuation marks, as a break in the sense in which the reader can pause. In this sense it should be as strong a break as any other punctuation mark except the full stop.

Semi-colon

This break in the sentence is weaker than a full stop and stronger than a comma. It indicates to the reader that he should not altogether forget the words that have appeared in the sentence so far, but he should be sure he has grasped their meaning before he goes on to read the rest. It is a versatile mark, and much undervalued. It is adequate to separate two independent clauses without a conjunction; it can also be used to separate two independent clauses with a conjunction, so that a reader who uses a semi-colon has no need to worry whether the word linking the clauses is a conjunction or an adverb.

A long sentence may be easier to follow if it is broken up into its main divisions by semi-colons and then into sub-divisions by commas.

Comma

This is a sign for the briefest pause. A pair of such pauses may be useful, as with these five words, to mark off a separate phrase or clause instead of brackets. It is not right to have one comma between a noun and its verb. Thus it would be wrong to say 'prices which the Government had expected to fall, rose.' But it is quite correct to have two commas, acting as brackets, between a subject and verb which are both outside the bracket. This would allow: 'prices, which the Government had expected to fall, rose.'

Brackets

Either round brackets or square brackets may serve to identify a phrase or clause within a sentence which can to some extent be understood if the part within the bracket is skipped. It is, so to speak, a footnote within the sentence. Such brackets may also be used to indicate that a longer passage, a sentence or group of sentences, is similarly skippable.

Dash

The trouble with the dash, —, is that it can be used to mean any other kind of punctuation mark; which makes it rather unhelpful. It is commonly used in pairs like other brackets, but since commas, round brackets and square brackets are available for this, it seems unnecessary for this purpose either. Most typewriters have no dash (the hyphen is different and shorter), and writing will usually be clearer if one of the other stops is used instead.

Quotation marks

These look the same as inverted commas. These two definitions express two different purposes, either to quote what someone else has said or written, or to draw attention in a special way to a word or words. Whether to use single quotation marks ('. . .') or double (" . . . "), is a matter of personal preference or house style. It is useful to have both when making a quotation within a quotation:

He said 'Lend me your copy of "Whitaker's Almanack"'.

Apostrophe

This is basically used to indicate that a letter or letters has been omitted, as in the poetical ' 'tis' (it is) or the colloquial 'don't'. Certain possessive pronouns which never had left anything out do not therefore have apostrophes: his, hers, its, theirs, ours, etc. The expression 'it is' is abbreviated to 'it's'.

The possessive apostrophe arose because at one stage in our history, instead of saying 'the book of Charles', people took the shorter and neater way of saying 'Charles his book'. Using the apostrophe to indicate that letters had been left out, this become 'Charles's book'. In time the suffix 's became attached to any noun as a way of displacing 'of', even where the apostrophe no longer represented any letters omitted. As a general rule words in the singular form the possessive by adding 's and words in the plural which do not end in s can add 's in the same way. Thus:

A woman's right.   Women's rights.

Even if the singular ends in s, as with Charles above, it is usually considered better to add 's as shown.

However, a plural ending in s conventionally adds no further s, but only the apostrophe after the final s. Thus:

The soldiers' uniforms.

The question mark

This is used, at the end of a sentence which is a question, in place of the full stop. Whether the sentence is a question or not depends strictly on the grammatical form it takes. So 'he asked whether it was likely' is a statement, and should not have a question mark at the end, although there is a question wrapped up in it. A request which takes the form of a question, as in 'Will you please fill up this form' should grammatically have a question mark at the end; but where the question does not require an answer, perhaps it is better to break the grammatical rule, and omit the question mark, than to make your reader wonder whether he is expected to say 'yes' or 'no'. It is more courteous, and more useful, to use a question mark if an answer is expected, but not otherwise.

Exclamation mark

This is used as a way of indicating in writing something spoken in heat, to indicate an emotional state of the speaker rather than a dry fact. In a report, if you quote somebody exclaiming, it is more correct and clearer to read if you put an exclamation mark instead of a full stop at the end.

Exclamation marks have, however, other uses in reports. It is useful to indicate clearly that a sentence is meant to be taken in a humorous or sarcastic or ironical way, if an exclamation mark is put at the end. For example: 'The Company Secretary issued a memorandum on ways of economizing in paper. The memorandum was four pages long!' It is the kind of observation which occurs somewhat rarely in reports, and since the reader is not expecting it, the writer needs to emphasize somehow that it is a joke, and the exclamation mark serves this purpose.

Appendix 3: a checklist for more effective writing

The checklist below derives from the ideas in this book augmented by those of the National Consumer Council and the Plain English Campaign. It aims to help the reader achieve clear, precise and effective writing. The points are not presented in any order of merit or importance and they apply to all report writing.

1 It is difficult to read a mixture of figures (14, 16.9) and words (twenty four million).
2 Do not mix decimals and fractions.
3 A logical tree, sometimes called an algorithm, is better than the same ideas expressed in prose, or even in a table.
4 Put the information in a sentence in the sequence which enables the reader to understand it most easily, and do not refer in the middle of the sentence to lists etc elsewhere.
5 Use ordinary language, not officialese.
6 Avoid using capital letters. In large quantities they are difficult to read, and tend to give an unsympathetic impression.
7 Let the typography and the layout of your prose emphasize clearly what are the main headings and clauses and what are the sub-clauses.
8 Vary the type size to establish logical priorities, and the differing importance of different sections.
9 Try to minimize or avoid definitions, or have a separate section for them.
10 Use short words rather than long ones.
11 Remember the emotional consequences of the words and typography you use. Do not threaten your reader.
12 Avoid headings which are irrelevant to the reader.
13 Avoid headings which are long-winded or depressing.
14 Put in any punctuation necessary.
15 Leave out any punctuation not necessary.
16 Minimize the use of numbering and lettering, but when doing

so, follow a consistent and meaningful system. Be consistent in the use of units.

17 Avoid vague headings like 'additional requirements'.

18 Avoid repeating simple instructions, as though the readers were particularly idiotic.

19 Consider the emotional strain, attitude, and expectations of those reading the report.

20 Avoid a string of subordinate clauses with complex inter-relations.

Appendix 4: bibliography

Words:

Oxford Paperback Dictionary, Oxford University Press.

Roget's Thesaurus, Pan Books Limited.

Style:

FOWLER, H W (revised by GOWERS, Sir Ernest), *Modern English Usage*, Oxford University Press.

GOWERS, Sir Ernest (revised by FRASER, Sir Bruce) *The Complete Plain Words*, Penguin.

VERNON, Tom, *Gobbledegook*, National Consumer Council, 1980.

Structure and style:

For technical reports: COOPER, Bruce, *Writing Technical Reports*, Penguin.

For accountants or commercial reports: FLETCHER, John and GOWING, David, *Effective Writing for Accountants*, The Institute of Chartered Accountants in England and Wales, 1979.

The Plain English Campaign, 78 Wiltshire Street, Salford M7 0BD, has been re-designing forms for public bodies and has issued a training kit for use in courses on form design.

Index

68